The Great Little
PLYMOUTH
Book

Chips Barber
Sally Barber

Illustrations:
Jane Reynolds

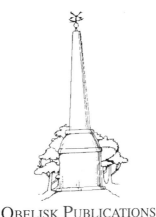

OBELISK PUBLICATIONS

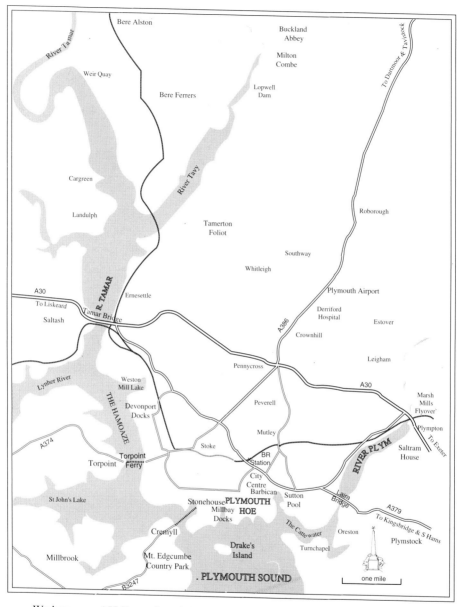

one mile

We have over 150 Devon-based titles – for a list of current books please write to us at 2 Church Hill, Pinhoe, Exeter, EX4 9ER telephone (01392) 468556

First published in 1991, reprinted in 1997 by
Obelisk Publications, 2 Church Hill, Pinhoe, Exeter, Devon
Designed by Chips and Sally Barber
Sketch map based on an out-of-copyright source
Printed in Great Britain by The Devonshire Press Ltd, Torquay, Devon

Plymouth has the biggest population of any settlement in Devon and in many respects is the most important. A glance at an index of a large atlas will reveal that the original Plymouth has given birth to many other 'Plymouths' throughout the world. It has been a place where people have been going from or coming back to for many centuries. It is this which has shaped its history and made it a famous name throughout the world. But it is more than that for it is a place in its own right, not just a destination or a point of departure. It has its old and new bits and perhaps even those bits it would rather do without! It is a working town and, if anyone takes the trouble to look, it is a good place to be. This has been borne out in recent years through surveys.

Having written *The Great Little Dartmoor, Exeter and Totnes Books*, I know that there is an interest in the local environment. People seem to like the recipe of light history mixed with a liberal sprinkling of anecdotes and observations.

Therefore it is hoped that *The Great Little Plymouth Book* will live up to expectations and that it will at least reflect some of Plymouth's flavour and colour.

We start at the interface between Plymouth old and Plymouth new.

St Andrew's, on Royal Parade, has played its part in Plymouth's history. This large church is 185 feet long and 96 feet wide and its tower, so much a feature of the Plymouth skyline, rises to 136 feet high. During the wartime blitz it was devastated leaving just the towers and the walls. A board was placed there by a local headmistress, Miss Margaret Smith, and on it was written a single word in Latin – 'Resurgam' – meaning 'I will rise again' and St Andrew's has done just that.

It has been rebuilt and forms part of an important and imposing line of buildings along the south side of Royal Parade with the Guildhall, Civic Centre and Theatre Royal completing a heavyweight line up.

Catherine of Aragon is featured in a window at the nearby Guildhall. As a sixteen-year-old, the bride of Prince Arthur knelt at St Andrew's to give thanks for her safe arrival from Spain. Little did she know that within a decade she was to be widowed, then to become Henry VIII's first, but longest reigning, queen.

Locals often refer to St Andrew's quite simply as 'the old church'. On 30 November 1957, appropriately St Andrew's Day, it was officially re-consecrated and re-opened. Visitors will no doubt notice a stark contrast from the peace of the church to the never-ending sound of traffic outside. A really striking feature of the church is its beautiful windows which are most colourful, as indeed are those of the Guildhall.

You could hardly fail to miss the Guildhall – the Luftwaffe certainly didn't! During the 1941 Blitz it suffered such extensive damage that only its shell survived. As Plymouth's fourth Guildhall it was built between 1870–1874 and it is a startling statistic to note that it cost ten times more to rebuild it than it originally cost!

In relation to its size, Plymouth was one of the worst bombed of British settlements. The heartache of losing twenty thousand buildings, twenty four schools, eight cinemas, one hundred pubs, six hotels and forty two churches is fully understandable and should never be forgotten.

The Guildhall is a magnificent municipal building. Its windows recount the history of Plymouth: featured is the attack on the town by the Bretons who, in 1403, razed six hundred homes to the ground; in another window Drake can be seen bringing water to the town; whilst other characters like William Cookworthy, founder of the china clay industry, appear elsewhere. The windows are another reminder that Plymouth is steeped in history and there is much about the Guildhall to reflect the city's past.

Nearby, where Armada Way passes under Royal Parade, is a subway which is a favoured location of buskers. If you stop to listen awhile you may take the opportunity to peruse the modern mural which lines the sides of the subway walls. It is yet another proud proclamation of the city's past, and key moments and characters are chronologically depicted from the days of Henry VII right through to the Task Force in the Falklands confrontation. The latter was of special significance to Plymouth because of its continuing links with the Royal Navy and the Royal Marines. The artwork is colourful and the mural enlivens some otherwise dull, dreary walls.

At the point where Notte Street bisects Armada Way is a tangible souvenir of Plymouth's naval links. It is the massive anchor which once restrained the HMS *Ark Royal*. It was presented to the City of Plymouth by the Admiral of the Fleet, on behalf of the Admiralty Board, on 28 April 1980.

The area immediately to the west of the Guildhall, if you discount the Law Courts and the Civic Centre, is that part of Plymouth which has become its entertainment centre, with a number of establishments geared to bring a little escapism into our lives.

The most obvious is the Theatre Royal where some well known faces such as John Nettles (*Bergerac*) and Des O'Connor have appeared in pantomime (oh no they haven't ... oh yes they have!). The theatre was opened in 1982 and, in name, replaces an earlier theatre which seated 1,192 people.

The earlier Theatre Royal was built between 1811–13 to the designs of John Foulston, a celebrated architect who was responsible for many fine buildings and terraces in Plymouth, some of which are but a stone's throw away. In June 1878 a terrible fire caused much damage to Foulston's theatre and, although it was rebuilt, it was eventually demolished in 1937 to be replaced by the Royal Cinema, later to become the ABC.

Other cinemas have their place in this, the Derry's Cross area of Plymouth. Among them is the Drake Cinema which was founded by 20th Century Fox, a rare occurrence for them. To celebrate its opening its first film was 'The Plymouth Story' a tribute to the people of Plymouth. At this 'premiere' (for the cinema) in 1958, two young celebrities were introduced, in person, to the audience – Jackie Collins and Richard Todd.

Nearby are the studios of the local television company TSW whose workers have, in the past, been troubled by ghosts. It is believed that the studios are built on a hospital burial ground which was reserved for French prisoners of war. As there have been less sightings in recent years, perhaps it is possible that they have gone home on the Cross-Channel ferry service to Roscoff!

There is great rivalry between the independent sector and the BBC. The latter now have studios in the Mannamead area but once had premises in what was Athenaeum Lane – the car park of TSW. However the BBC have maintained a presence in the area as Radio Devon occupies studios in Catherine Street.

The line up of entertainment buildings has been completed, in 1991, by the addition of the Pavilions. Occupying the site of the ill-fated 'bubbles' this new structure offers ice skating and swimming facilities. It is a venue ideally designed to stage shows with top stars and performing artists who draw big audiences. Its own history has just begun.

At the back of the Theatre Royal is a clock tower, one of the oldest of many in Devon. This is Derry's Clock, named after former mayor William Derry who gave it to the city in 1862. In its early days locals referred to it as 'the four faced deceiver' because it has a fountain on each side but no water! It was originally intended to locate this clock tower at Cornwall Street Gate, but fate decreed it should be where it is and, ironically, when almost everything which had surrounded it has gone, it survives. Indeed, when the present Theatre Royal was being constructed, Derry's Clock was completely boxed up to afford it protection.

Beside Derry's Clock is a most unusual pub. It is called 'the Bank', an apt name as that is precisely what it was in the past. The change from solid to liquid assets took quite a time, but the conversion has been a success and the Bank has a regular clientele from the nearby shops, cinemas, theatres, offices and

real banks. Although I enquired of the staff as to the Bank's history, I was met with a wall of blank expression. The one thing the bar staff were sure about was a ghost deep in the bowels of the dark, cool cellar which they hadn't seen, but they felt the 'spirit' was all around. However, further research revealed that the Bank was designed by Charles Robert Cockerell (1788–1863), who was a London architect with a partiality to the design of English Baroque, and it is built in a material called rusticated ashlar. The Wiltshire and Dorset Bank were the first incumbents until it became a branch of 'Lloyds'. Sadly its rotating door has now gone but, perhaps, it's just as well as some of the more inebriated patrons might have got trapped and spent all night going around and around!

It was certainly some stout and sober people who were responsible for the layout of the modern city centre, with its tidy pattern of symmetrical streets. However there are various schools of thought about Plymouth's city centre. The old school hark back to and hanker for the halcyon days when there was less uniformity in both the layout of the streets and a greater variety in the architecture and ownership of shops. And there are the more recent generations who live in blissful ignorance of the 'colourful' city that went before, who have grown up on the comfortably wide thoroughfares and who have, in more recent times, grown accustomed to traffic-free shopping areas. This aspect has to be welcomed – Plymouth formerly suffered terrible traffic problems. In common with most old towns, pre-war Plymouth made no allowance for the rigours and demands of modern traffic flow.

Nobody, however, would have sanctioned the method which led to the changes brought about. The blitz on central Plymouth was devastating and ripped its heart right out; little was left standing where a bustling town once thrived. Although there had long been talk of necessary change, nobody had contemplated that this would be forced on them and nobody could have conceived the scale on which that change would be.

Most of the work for the re-building of Plymouth was undertaken by Sir Patrick Abercrombie, a planning expert, and Mr Paton Watson, the City Engineer. This was a rare opportunity to create something new and exciting, where the traffic could flow more freely and, more importantly, there was an opportunity to link the city centre with the Hoe, both directly and visually. This was something not considered possible in the old town, but the end product is 'Armada Way', a wide, spacious avenue of about a thousand yards.

Even though the German bombs had razed the city centre to the ground, the 'Plan for Plymouth' still necessitated the clearance of many thousands of terraced homes first. Needless to say, there were those who survived Hitler's bombs only to be shell-shocked at the changes brought about by our own civilian planners in post-war Plymouth!

In the 1980s it was considered an important task to mellow the stark appearance of the grid-iron pattern of streets and the all too rectangular, cuboid look of many of the buildings. The landscaping which has been cleverly executed has added colour and softness to the main shopping area. By pedestrianising these streets it has created a more relaxed atmosphere. The man-made waterway, the fountains, the paving and above all the wonderful use of flowers has combined to make the once bustling, even hectic, centre a place where the quality of life for the shopper has been greatly improved. If only the prevailing wind could be managed with such expertise!

Dotted around the edge of the city centre are a number of historic buildings which are well worth a visit, but which are often missed by those on a flying visit to Plymouth.

One of these is the Prysten House which, as its name suggests, was once a lodging place for priests. However, when the Priory of Plympton was suppressed the building saw some very different secular residents, even though the locals still referred to it as 'the Abbey':

for a while a band of smugglers made it their den; later a wealthy wine merchant took up residence; then a family of grocers moved in. The latter, in successive generations, stayed for one hundred and fifty years and managed to blacken the roofs whilst in the process of smoking and curing hams.

During the renovation and restoration of this historic home amazing discoveries were made – hidden staircases were found concealed within thick walls and long-forgotten windows and doorways were revealed. Less exciting was a layer of fat, more than half an inch thick, lining a wall which had been plastered over!

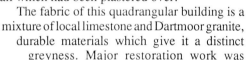

The fabric of this quadrangular building is a mixture of local limestone and Dartmoor granite, durable materials which give it a distinct greyness. Major restoration work was carried out in the 1950s, but it was not until 1976 that it was opened to the public on a regular basis.

The building is located at the back of St Andrew's Church, at the top of Finewell Street. This street's name, however apt, has nothing to do with the magistrates court which is sited near here, but is named after a well! It was one of several that served the town until the population grew too large. That was the point when Sir Francis Drake agreed to engineer a new supply from Dartmoor.

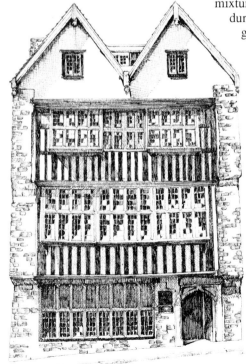

Nearby is the Merchant House Museum which was restored by the Plymouth City Council between 1972 and 1977. At one time its surroundings were more in keeping with its appearance and scale for there was an old lodging house on one side and an inn on the other. The house was built for James Parker, a celebrated Elizabethan sea captain who, like Drake, was also a Mayor of Plymouth. The building has been used for a variety of purposes including a shop and a cobbler's. It is worth a visit to discover much of Plymouth's past through its excellent displays.

On reaching the remnants of Charles Church, in the middle of its irregularly shaped roundabout, most visitors to Plymouth will wonder what it is doing there and why it is in that condition. The answers lie on an informative notice board near the entrance to a subway, but as most people drive speedily past on the inner city racetrack they miss the details.

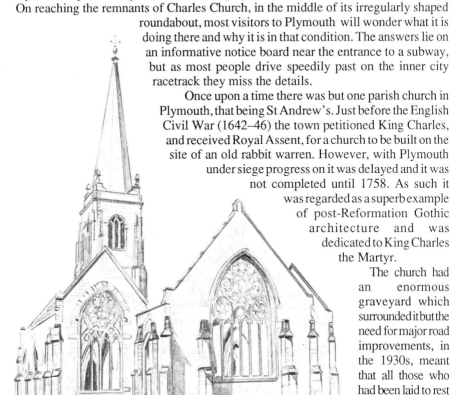

Once upon a time there was but one parish church in Plymouth, that being St Andrew's. Just before the English Civil War (1642–46) the town petitioned King Charles, and received Royal Assent, for a church to be built on the site of an old rabbit warren. However, with Plymouth under siege progress on it was delayed and it was not completed until 1758. As such it was regarded as a superb example of post-Reformation Gothic architecture and was dedicated to King Charles the Martyr.

The church had an enormous graveyard which surrounded it but the need for major road improvements, in the 1930s, meant that all those who had been laid to rest had to be removed. Then, during the Second World War, this church was gutted by fire on the night of 21 March 1941. Following the war it lay in ruins for many years and became a potentially dangerous landmark. The ecclesiastical powers-that-be decided against rebuilding it so the Plymouth Corporation acquired the land and the Ministry of Works rendered it safe. Now it is a memorial to the suffering endured during the many enemy air attacks on the city.

A short distance away is a part of Plymouth which is revered by many as the best area of the city. The Barbican is that part which visitors are drawn to because it is different. Whereas almost every city centre today is predictable in its types of shops and businesses, the Barbican is something of a surprise package. It is certainly a place which should be explored. It is a maze of claustrophobic streets and back-alleys; it is the home of an independently-minded community; it is a place of talent and endeavour with many artists and craftsmen plying their trades in the 'village' within a city; and at night it is a lively and colourful place. Retired Plymouth police constables will tell many a tale of their experiences of this lively night life – some of which would make your hair curl!

In the Merchant House Museum there is the old Barbican Ducking Stool. The last 'client' was an old fisherwoman called Nancy Clark whose punishment was meted out because of her inability to curb her tongue. She was known to express her feelings with outbursts of obscene language and, when challenged, she was prone to become physically aggressive and accustomed assault on anyone within immediate striking distance. It seems a little strange that it was acceptable to 'dunk undesirables' off the Barbican Quay when it was illegal to deposit dogs, fish, flesh, cats, pigs or 'deaded' beasts from the spot!

The Barbican has plenty of wining and dining places, the need for these dating back to the days when many a thirsty sailor descended on the place after months away at sea. It was not uncommon for Sutton Pool to be filled to capacity with visiting craft: occasionally there would be two hundred or more Cornish luggers up from West Cornwall; there were the Scottish fishermen with their skilled fish wives who could cure herrings, and process most fish with consummate skill; and there were the sailors from all over the world. The local 'ladies' were a durable breed and gave a good account of themselves in the face of overwhelming adversity ... so it is said. The church tried to provide the fishermen with more sober activities, so draughts and dominoes were popular distractions whilst the fishermen smoked pigtails of tobacco.

Historically the Barbican has been of National and world-wide importance. It became important in

Elizabethan times. Sir Francis Drake lived close to Sutton Harbour, in Looe Street, prior to acquiring Buckland Abbey. Sir Walter Raleigh is believed to have resided even nearer, at 12 Notte Street. Robert Lenkiewicz's mural on the Parade depicts an Elizabethan scene – a colourful personal interpretation by a man of great talent who has lead an unusual life. On Southside Street is another of his masterpieces which shows an assembly of healthy people who are not dressed as Elizabethans – in fact they are not dressed at all!

At the junction of Black Friars Lane and Southside Street is one of Plymouth's attractions, a distillery which makes Plymouth Dry Gin. In the season it is possible to have not only an audio-visual show but also a guided tour. You may learn some fascinating facts – the Dutch invented gin and served it up to troops waiting to go into battle, it helped calm their nerves and from this we have the expression 'Dutch Courage'. In addition to a promising future, the building has a colourful history. It is the city's oldest remaining building (1383) and has been used for a diverse number of purposes. In 1536 it was a debtor's prison, it then became the first religious meeting place for non-conformists. It is believed that the Pilgrim Fathers held their final meeting here before setting sail in 1620. Plymouth Gin was first produced at Black Friars in 1793 and, some two centuries on, it produces about four million bottles each year (half of which are vodka).

Opposite this distillery is the old pannier market which is typical of the unusual type of shop in this the oldest part of Plymouth. In the Barbican area there are many other off-street shopping malls and arcades where you may purchase 'something different'.

The pavements of Southside Street are particularly noticeable on dull wet days when they shine with great colour. These local stones are pinky grey but streaked with vivid red and pink to make an eye-catching spectacle.

At one time Sutton Pool was a more extensive sheet of water. It was a favoured haven because it was sheltered from the prevailing wind by the high ridge of the Hoe and it also enjoyed a big tidal range.

The low tides however often revealed a less pleasant side of this inlet. The original settlement grew around the pool and, quite naturally, it became the means of disposal for raw sewage. In Elizabethan times this was referred to as 'gumphus' but by 1882, when some thirty thousand tons of it had accumulated, more familiar words were used to describe the awful stench and sight which occurred at every low water. This gave rise to a popular activity, around 1900, when children would gather where the sewage drain entered into Sutton Pool to wait for the human waste, which creates a lot of natural gas, to build up, behind the flap controlling the flow, and explode!

With reclamation projects and the need for more warehouses, Sutton Pool has shrunk to much smaller dimensions than it was originally. Its functions have also changed and continue to do so. Many of the maritime orientated activities, which were conducted amidst a hive of great activity, around the harbour have gone. Warehouses of great height have undertaken new roles as luxury flats, wine lodges, health clubs, restaurants, workshops and so on.

The Custom House which looks down onto the north west corner of Sutton Harbour was opened in 1820, its magnificent clock arriving some three years later. Next door is the Three Crowns, one of Plymouth's oldest pubs which is nearly four hundred years old. The external frontage has not altered greatly in that time but any old 'sea salt' coming back to haunt the place might not recognise the interior.

The earlier Custom House is on the opposite side of the road and it has remained in tact despite Hitler's attempts, and other local plans, to demolish it.

Much of the Barbican area of Plymouth is genuinely old and for this we should be thankful as would-be developers, in all shapes and sizes, have eyed up the various possibilities of clearing away old buildings. But various local associations, preservationists and conservationists have united on a number of occasions to oppose and thwart wholesale changes.

New Street is not new at all – it is the oldest street in Plymouth! It was built and developed by John Sparke. When it was new it went under the name of 'Rag Street', and remained so until 1746. It was a prosperous street with many celebrated and wealthy families in residence there, families which have played a considerable part in the life and history of Devon. However, as Plymouth prospered and the population swelled, the gentry gradually moved out and were replaced with large numbers of less affluent folk. The street lost its classy image and began to deteriorate.

One of the more important houses in New Street is Number 32, the Elizabethan House. In 1929 a committee entrusted with the task of preserving old Plymouth saved the building from demolition and, in more recent years, it has become a museum, reflecting the mood and life of its period. One clever touch is the way the staircase negotiates a ship's mast.

The Barbican, with all its old buildings, is thought to have a number of ghosts. The most interesting of these was a 'daylight' ghost that was once so regular in its appearances that it drew large crowds. It would be seen high on the side of a building, paying no heed to all the onlookers. Alas this Edwardian spook has not appeared in recent years, possibly because his 'old haunt' has now changed so much!

A short distance away from New Street is the Mayflower Steps. The history of many parts of the world has been influenced by the various comings and goings at or near this spot. Americans, in particular, are conscious of the significance of this point, where many of their ancestors gathered to begin the transatlantic adventure which helped to shape the development of their country.

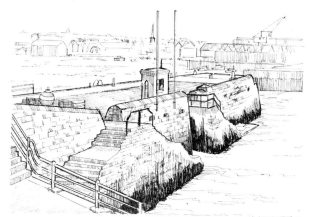

Film-makers have tried to convey the problems and perils faced by the 162 Pilgrim Fathers who set sail on the *Mayflower* but *Halliwell's*

Film Guide is less than kind about Spencer Tracy's film version of this historic voyage. Called 'Plymouth Adventure' it is described as a 'well-meaning schoolbook history, totally unconvincing and very dull despite obvious effort all round.' Another critic added that 'It demonstrates how Hollywood can dull down as well as jazz up history'. Reality was austere and those who sailed from Plymouth did so out of sheer desperation to escape both religious and financial problems. It was very much a last throw of the dice in the Game of Life for an assembly of people from far and wide who had been oppressed and persecuted for a great many years.

Plymouth's links with the Pilgrim Fathers are not as strong as one might imagine. Initially they had no intention of putting into Plymouth but when their first attempt at a transatlantic crossing failed they sought sanctuary here. They arrived in Plymouth on 5 August and set sail for the New World on 6 September 1620. A month of refuge, safe from persecution, has lead to an everlasting link between Plymouth and the Pilgrim Fathers.

Their destination was Virginia but Atlantic storms blew them well off course and instead they landed much further north at a point near Cape Cod. Amazingly, and by coincidence, the spot where they set foot in the New World had already been named by Captain John Smith, some six years earlier, as Plymouth!

Near the Mayflower Steps is Island House where some of the Pilgrims were accommodated. On the outside is a board which lists all their names – it replaces an earlier one which only listed the menfolk! The Pilgrims, or 'Saints' as they were known, were not only non-conformists in their beliefs and religious practices but also in their names. For instance there was Love Brewster, Remember Allerton, Resolved White and Humility Cooper. On that fateful journey in 1620 one passenger died and two were born. These were given the appropriate names of 'Oceanus' Hopkins and 'Peregrine' White (Peregrine means pilgrim).

The one hundred and eighty ton *Mayflower* was an old ship about ninety feet long and the ship's company was made up of Pilgrims and others who were without religious convictions but who simply wanted a new life in the New World.

Other tangible links are Plymouth Argyle, the local soccer team, is known as the Pilgrims and Plymouth's Leisure Centre in Central Park is the Mayflower Sports Centre. The line of eighteen colourful flags on the Hoe were put up in 1970 as part of the 350th anniversary celebrations of the Mayflower's departure.

On 20 April 1957 a replica of the Mayflower (made at Uphams

Yard at Brixham) set sail from Plymouth. Their epic journey took thirteen days less than the original and there was no attempt made to authenticate or re-enact the hardships or difficulties experienced in 1620.

The pier on which the Mayflower Steps are located was the work of John MacBride, a man who rose to Admiral and who lead a full life, including representing Plymouth as a Member of Parliament for six years. He supervised the building of the pier which enabled Sutton Pool to be more sheltered.

Here are a great number of plaques which recount many significant historic arrivals or departures. One commemorates the arrival home, in 1837, of four of the Tolpuddle Martyrs, Thomas and John Stanfield, James Brind and James Loveless, from Australia's Botany Bay. A quicker journey was enjoyed by the first transatlantic flight when the seaplane, NC4, touched down on 31 May 1919. Amongst people leaving was Captain

James Cook who sailed for Australia and whose explorations provided much new geographical knowledge. In likewise fashion Humphrey Gilbert set sail for Newfoundland, Richard Grenville for Virginia, and Thomas Stuckley for Florida.

From the Barbican to the Hoe is a long, slow climb. On the right, the imposing Citadel is a towering bastion of limestone masonry whilst, on the left, is an ever-changing picture as the Plym enters Plymouth Sound.

All around is a scene of activity with all sorts of vessels, large and small, either leaving or entering the mouth of the Plym, known as the Cattewater. Experts have disagreed over the meaning of this peculiar place name. In the thirteenth century the estuary was simply called 'the Catte'. Possibly the name is a legacy from the times when the Danes invaded these shores a few centuries earlier as, in their own part of the world, they have the Kattegat, the strait between Sweden and Denmark.

The Marine Biological Association is an establishment whose work is the sea. Sited beside the Citadel it has investigated, for more than a century, the state of marine ecology around our shores. The information it has accumulated has been of use to many organisations and to those whose occupations have a vested interest in the sea. There is also an aquarium which houses many of the marine species indigenous to British coastal waters and this is open to the public at certain times.

'Plymouth Hoe' is famous throughout the world! Almost everyone has heard of it yet only a small proportion of its many visitors appreciate its importance. We start first with its geology for it is nature which throws up this wonderful vantage point over Plymouth Sound. 'Hoe' is a Saxon word which means a projecting ridge of land but most people prefer to interpret it as meaning 'high place'. It is a limestone cliff which rises sharply to about one hundred and fifty feet high before bevelling out to a plateau surface. A century or two ago the cliff was a much more obvious feature but human intervention has meant that much landscaping and construction work has altered its face. However an observant visitor will be able to clearly visualise what these cliffs may have looked like had they not been sited at the northern end of one of the best natural harbours in the world. Limestone though has its uses and everywhere in Plymouth there are examples of walls, houses, buildings and bridges built in the local stone.

For a really good view of the surrounding area, climb to the top of Smeaton's lighthouse where (providing you don't suffer from vertigo) a reasonable time can

be devoted to scanning the far horizons. To the north east is Dartmoor, its unmistakable skyline a constant reminder that the National Park plays an important part in Plymothians' leisure time. On fine summer days there is a mass exodus to such spots as Shaugh Bridge and Cadover Bridge, both on the River Plym, and to Roborough Down. Visible from Smeaton's Tower on the Dartmoor skyline are distinctive white mounds, these are the spoil heaps of the China Clay industry of Lee Moor. Hopefully in time they will 'green over' and blend into the landscape.

In the opposite direction is Cornwall and, in particular, the Mount Edgcumbe Estate. This was officially a part of Devon until 1844 but now is part of that ancient kingdom of 'oggies' and 'emmets' (pasties and tourists). To the south and out to sea is the Breakwater. Television personality Anneka Rice began one of the *Treasure Hunt* series from here several years ago. In her helicopter quest to find five clues as directed by two 'blind' studio contestants there was much confusion as to the direction she should leave the comfortingly solid Breakwater. With much misgivings the helicopter was directed out to sea – but all turned out well when a submarine surfaced for her to land on!

The engineer of the Breakwater was Sir John Rennie. He undertook the task of building it in 1812 and closely followed its fortunes until it was completed some twenty-eight years later, in 1840. Estimates at the amount of stone needed to construct it vary considerably.

Millions of tons of limestone was taken from Oreston, a settlement on the opposite side of the Plym and now incorporated into Plymouth. Three million tons of Dartmoor granite was also used for the facings and eight hundred men were employed in the quarrying activities. The first stone was dropped into place by the Prince Regent (who later became George IV). The site for the Breakwater was chosen because the bed of Plymouth Sound had a series of underwater peaks or shoals and these submarine blisters were joined together and filled in. It made Plymouth a more sheltered harbour.

On the western end is a lighthouse which was built in 1844 and manned by three keepers until the summer of 1963, the year it was automated. Its warning light flashes white every ten seconds when seen from the Hoe, but when viewed from the Barbican, it is red! There was an intention to put an identical lighthouse on the eastern end, making it resemble a giant mantelpiece with 'candlesticks' at either end, but the effectiveness of the first one, and the cost involved, resulted in the placement of a pole bearing a cage which could be used, so it is said, by shipwrecked sailors. A close inspection of it will reveal that its design specification leaves a lot to be desired, one might be far safer chancing it with the mermaids!

Near the centre of the Breakwater is a fort which was part of Plymouth's fortifications in the 1860s. It is deceptively large and, at a pinch, could accommodate almost two hundred people. It was part of a massive scheme to protect Plymouth from a possible conflict with the French. The town was surrounded by a ring of forts which, because they were expensive and never saw military action in wartime, were known as 'Palmerston's Follies' after the Prime Minister of the day.

The Breakwater has enhanced the success of Plymouth as a port and there was a time when there was a procession of ocean going/coming passenger liners steaming past into Plymouth. However the real beneficiaries are the small boat owners who can enjoy the delights of the Sound which is a mill pond compared to the more rigorous waters just a few miles out in the Channel.

From the Hoe it is possible to spy the fourteen miles distant landmark of the Eddystone Lighthouse. If it is spied from atop Smeaton's Tower, then an invisible link is created as there is a small stump beside the Eddystone tower which is the original base of Smeaton's tower! Smeaton's Tower was one of several to stand on the Eddystone Reef and gave good service for well over a century between 1759 and 1877. Smeaton himself, a Yorkshireman, had to stand on the Hoe and look out to sea with a spyglass to see the opening ceremony as the weather was too bad for him to get out to the reef.

Smeaton's Tower was so well constructed that it would probably still be out on the reef had not the sea undermined its foundations to the extent that in the fiercest of storms it would rock alarmingly! A new lighthouse was built beside it and the hundreds of blocks forming Smeaton's Tower were numbered, dismantled, transported and reassembled on the Hoe.

Much has been written about all the lighthouses which have stood on the reef but a brief synopsis tells the story of the reef as follows.

After almost a shipwreck-a-day Henry Winstanley, an Essex merchant, inventor, magician and wit, engineered the first 'light' of sixty candles in November 1698. Almost five years to the day the worst storm of all time was predicted. Winstanley boasted his light would withstand it; he was so confident that he was rowed out so that he could experience nature's wildest elements. Alas he perished with his tower.

Cornish merchant John Rudyerd built the second tower of timber so that, like trees, it would give way to the wind but, after almost half a century, it burnt down. One of the keepers, Henry Hall, was ninety four years old. He climbed to inspect the burning light with mouth agape. However, the heat of the fire had melted the cupola and poor Henry swallowed a sizable chunk of molten material which, when it solidified, weighed almost half a pound. He survived several days during which time he told many people what had happened and no-one believed him until after he'd died and Dr Spry performed an autopsy on him.

The third tower was Smeaton's, whilst the fourth, and present day structure, was built by Mr J.N. Douglass. Like so many 'lights' now, it is automated; no longer do the keepers fish from the tower, using kites to carry their lines away.

In 1860 Smeaton's Tower was chosen to be on the back of the penny coin, a choice which was repeated in 1937. Obviously it proved a popular design because it held this honour until decimilization was introduced.

Smeaton's Tower has been painted in various colours throughout the years and, with the steady growth in Plymouth as a visitor centre, its spick and span appearance is in keeping with the clean and colourful image of the city. The attractive parks, gardens and flower beds are another feature of the Hoe area. The splashes of colour help to disguise the drab nature of the native grey limestones.

The wide open space of the Hoe has played host to many shows, exhibitions, parades and gatherings, a veritable cocktail of activities. When the National Armada Memorial was unveiled on 21 October 1890, it was an event reported widely in the national press. It was estimated that some sixty thousand people attended to cover almost every square inch of available space. The foundation stone for the monument was laid two years earlier to commemorate the 300th Anniversary of the first sighting of the 'Spanish Armada' from Plymouth Hoe. It also commemorates the Battle of Trafalgar, hence the date it was unveiled – Trafalgar Day! Atop the monument, Britannia presided over three hundred choristers whilst the bells of St Andrew's and St Charles rang out. Alfred, the Duke of Edinburgh performed the ceremony, and he made reference to the fact that he had visited the Hoe previously to lay the foundation stone for Smeaton's Tower.

Drake's statue is a simpler affair, based on the one which stands at Tavistock, his birthplace. Drake is now ever vigilant, protecting

Plymouth against any would-be invaders. The statue portrays him dressed in the smart attire of an Elizabethan gentleman, it is about ten feet tall, and is so appropriate as his contribution to the life and times of Elizabethan Plymouth cannot be overstated. The statue, by Sir Edgar Boehm, was unveiled in 1884 by Lady Eliott Fuller-Drake. Whilst the ceremony was being conducted she sat in a chair which was made from the ship's timbers of the *Golden Hind*! The chair is now housed in the Bodleian Library in Oxford. Needless to say vast crowds congregated for this colourful event.

Much is made of Drake's celebrated 'game of bowls' on Plymouth Hoe in 1588. He was probably involved in a game of bowls on a site which is now part of the Citadel, but there was logic to his casual, legendary, statement: 'There is time to win the game and beat the Spaniards too'. Drake knew that his fleet could do nothing with the tide and weather conditions against him. When he did put out to sea, his smaller ships, and therefore more manoeuvrable fleet, were able to defeat and disperse the enemy. The local bowling green has capitalised on this historic game of bowls in choosing its name.

Drake's exploits of war and conquest are well chronicled in the history books as is his circumnavigation of the world (1577–80). But some of his quieter, more domestic, achievements sometimes get overlooked. He was aware that the local water supply from wells sunk into the limestone were insufficient, so he set about bringing water from Dartmoor down to the town. For a fee of £300 Drake had to pay compensation to the landowners and finance the building of it. He cut the first sod in December 1590, and some four months later rode on horseback to accompany the first waters to flow the eighteen miles journey down from the River Meavy (at a point which is now the bed of Burrator Reservoir) to Plymouth. The need for this watercourse was amplified by local Victorian historian, Mrs Bray of Tavistock. She stated that there was such a shortage of water that Plymothians were obliged to send their dirty washing to Plympton! The Plymouth Leat, or Drake's Leat, served the city for a long time but today is disused. If you wish to walk along a stretch there are some good, dry sections on Roborough Down, but watch out for the occasional adder which may lurk in this trench!

The great central monument on Plymouth Hoe is another, lasting reminder of the city's connections with the sea. Rising one hundred feet skywards is the white stone monument of the Naval War Memorial which was designed by Sir Robert Lorimer. It is very much in keeping with similar memorials at the great naval towns of Portsmouth and Chatham. From the sea it is seen as an imposing silhouette against the skyline. On its bronze panels, situated between its four lions, are scenes of naval action from the war, a time when some seven thousand officers and men of the Plymouth Division lost their lives at sea, whilst nearby is a memorial to the many soldiers who also perished.

So far we have talked largely about Plymouth Hoe in relation to its monuments, but it is very much a place of the people. During the last war, when the bombs rained down on the city wreaking death and destruction, the people of Plymouth surfaced to visit the Hoe en masse to dance there. This was an act of defiance to Hitler, a show of unity and corporate spiritedness and a way of relieving the great stress to which they were all subjected.

For many years Plymothians have availed themselves of the opportunities afforded to them by the waters of the Sound. The hardy (and the foolhardy!) have often braved the elements to swim at Tinside, either in the pool or in the sea. To them this was 'Tinside on Sea' and they revelled in the less than warm sea water. There were groups of stalwart swimmers who formed 'clubs' to participate in all the year round bathing. There was the 'Seven o'clock Regulars', 'the Tinside Champions' and the 'Shackey Pool Stragglers' all who would have appreciated the improvements made to the facilities in 1913.

There was also those daring young men of the 'naughty nineties' who, a century ago, cavorted and romped around in the nude, much to the dismay of some but to the delight of others! However, these fun-loving frollickers had to keep a safe distance, high on the promenade, when the Ladies, complete with modest attire took to the water. For one special race about twenty five men took on a theme which resulted in 'Mr Almond', 'Mr Beech', 'Mr Chestnut', and 'Miss Coconut' being assisted by 'A Big Nut', 'What a Nut' and 'A Regular Nut'. Needless to say the race was started by 'The Kernel'! There are not quite as many 'nuts' around today but there are a number of people who ritualistically swim every day of the year.

The 'New Sea Water Bathing Pool' was opened on 2 October 1935 at 7.00 pm and the occasion was celebrated by a night of aquatic comedy.

Then there are those people who, although they like to commune with the sea, prefer not to enter it but instead savour its sea airs. In 1884 Plymothians could stroll a hundred and fifty yards or so out over the water on the new 'Promenade Pier' which projected out into the water below the Belvedere. It was a banjo-shaped pier which cost £45,000 and

initially concentrated on offering band music to promenaders. In 1891 the bandstand was replaced by an elaborate two thousand-seater Pavilion and a range of entertainments were run which included concert parties, roller skating and wrestling. Designed by Mr E. Burch, a Londoner, the pier was both a financial and social success. Perhaps its most unusual feature was the cast iron seats which bore the shape of dolphins. Sadly this most popular of landmarks became a victim of the war and the only way to see it now is on old black and white photographs or postcards and the occasional archive cine-film. The passenger ferries now come in under the Hoe where the pier once stood so elegantly. However, the road which runs from the Millbay direction up to the Hoe is still called Pier Street.

Another place of entertainment which gave pleasure to so many people was the Hoe Summer Theatre, a prefabricated structure. It was built in 1962 to replace a large marquee and for twenty years it accommodated a wide range of shows, plays and performances. Some famous acts 'trod the boards' there and I can fondly remember going to see 'Goodie' Tim Brooke-Taylor star in a comedy a short time before it closed its doors for the last time, to be demolished and become an open space once more.

But life goes on and all around are the sights and sounds of people enjoying an ice cream, a swim in Tinside Pool, a sunbathe on one of the many terraces or perhaps a short cruise on one of the pleasure boats.

The Plymouth Dome, just below Smeaton's Tower, is without doubt the best way to get an appreciation of Plymouth's history. Within this

imaginative, modern building is all the brilliant audio-visual equipment needed to portray Plymouth's past. Assembled here are wonderful sight, sound and smell experiences which will excite and educate visitors. In 1989 it was voted 'the best new attraction in the UK' and a journey back through Plymouth's history can be as short, or as long, as you want.

From the viewing area of the Dome there is an excellent vista of Plymouth Sound. Drake's Island, previously called St Nicholas Island and prior to that St Michael's (both patron saints of fishermen), was once a most important place. In the Civil War it was a vital part of the Parliamentarians' grip on Plymouth.

Sir Alexander Carew was put in charge of the island but his suspicious behaviour caused his men to realise that he was really for the Royalists. They, bravely, arrested him and a year later he was beheaded in London.

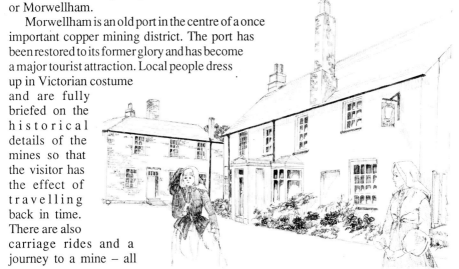

The island has served Plymouth as a State prison, as a fort, and an adventure centre where canoeing and abseiling were important activities.

Drake moored here, on his return from his major voyage, whilst he wisely sent a representative into Plymouth to find out if Elizabeth was still on the throne.

Slightly further along the Hoe is a tiered building which is landscaped into the side of the hill. This is the Belvedere which derives its name from the Italian words which translate into 'fine view'. Its date is clearly marked – 1891. On the road beneath it was once a bull-ring where animals which were scheduled for slaughter at the 'Shambles Market' (close to St Andrew's) were tethered. For obvious reasons this construction has been nicknamed 'the Wedding Cake'.

Nearby the plaintiff cries of cruise operators fill the air in the summer season. Their repetitive invitations to 'see the Dockyards and the Warships' on an hour long cruise are usually persuasive enough to woo enough passengers. Apart from this hour-long adventure there are also two hour voyages past the Breakwater and around the coastline to the Yealm Estuary or up the Tamar to Calstock and/ or Morwellham.

Morwellham is an old port in the centre of a once important copper mining district. The port has been restored to its former glory and has become a major tourist attraction. Local people dress up in Victorian costume and are fully briefed on the historical details of the mines so that the visitor has the effect of travelling back in time. There are also carriage rides and a journey to a mine – all just a journey up the River Tamar. If you do this voyage you will be following in the wake of Queen Victoria who went up river in 1856 to visit the Duke of Bedford at his home at Endsleigh. Her patronage of the river was largely instrumental in opening up the valley for pleasure steamer trips – at its peak of prosperity one hundred thousand people per year enjoyed the cruises. Today only a fraction of that number go on such a cruise but it is still the best way to see the valley!

The Royal Citadel dominates the eastern end of Plymouth Hoe, a colourless building with a contrastingly colourful past! It is entirely fitting that Plymouth should possess such magnificent fortifications. The twenty five feet thick limestone walls have ramparts which extend for over half a mile. Plymouth has been a target for many would-be conquerors yet, so far, the Citadel, imposing and unfussy, has stood sentinel over the City in its role of protector.

In its time though, it has not only protected Plymouth, but has also protected the King's interests and kept an eye on Plymothians! As we have already seen, they were staunch in their support of the Parliamentarian cause during the Civil War and this edifice, constructed less than two decades later, enabled Charles II to sleep a bit more soundly! He visited Plymouth in 1671 and again in 1677 to see for himself this fine building which is a wonderful example of English Baroque, designed by the King's chief military

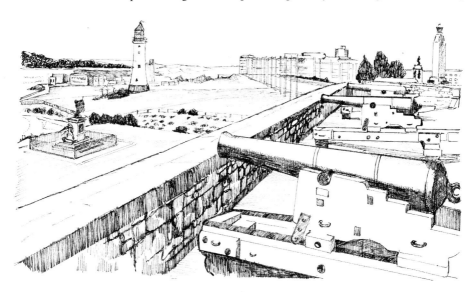

engineer, Bernard de Gomme. Most of the stone used in its construction was taken from a quarry on the western flank of the Hoe. Today it has been landscaped into West Hoe Park and its former purpose is generally well disguised by an avenue of tall cypress trees, various evergreens and shrubs.

Within the Citadel is the Royal Garrison Chapel of St Katherine-upon-the-Hoe, the 'Royal' by courtesy of George V in 1927. The chapel was built in 1668 but rebuilt in 1845 in a Gothic Style. A place of worship had existed on or near this site for centuries. In the Citadel is an Argentinian 155 mm gun which was brought back from Port Stanley, in the Falkland Isles, in 1982. The Citadel is well worth a visit and hour long summer time tours are organised by the Plymouth Regional Guides Association.

The Mount Edgcumbe Estate, which looks invitingly close when viewed from the heights of Plymouth Hoe, is a drive, via the Torpoint Ferry, of about twelve miles. A more direct link to the Cornish side of the estuary can be made by boarding 'The Northern Belle'

(the Cremyll Ferry). It runs twice hourly, each way, in summer but only hourly in the winter, from the Admiral's Hard in Stonehouse across to Cremyll. And, hey presto, the undeniable beauties of the Mount Edgcumbe Country Park lie at your feet with no charge to roam the gardens and extensive parkland. Should you wish to visit the house there is an entrance fee. It was rebuilt following its gutting by a stray incendiary bomb which had been intended for Devonport Docks, a mile away. The fabric of the building remained largely intact and architect Adrian Gilbert Scott has cleverly recreated this beautiful home for the Earls of Mount Edgcumbe.

The country park rises to the elevated Maker Heights, crowned by Maker Church, and is blessed by tremendous views over Plymouth Sound. For the lazy and the laid back who simply wish to relax there are the formal gardens of floral splendour. Lady Sophia, wife of the second Earl, was responsible for the Italian and French Gardens which benefit from the shelter given by enormous hedges. The Orangery is now a place for refreshments, a light spacious and beautiful building, which reputedly grew the best oranges in the kingdom – it is likely that no less than five English monarchs may have savoured these fruits. Mount Edgcumbe was famed throughout Europe for its beauty – Duke Medina Sidonia, who was the leader of the Spanish Armada, earmarked the estate as his personal trophy in his victory over the English! Fortunately it never came to that and the likes of Samuel Pepys, the great diarist, have since been able to note the delights of this sheltered jewel of the landscape.

There is a folly on the steep open sward overlooking Plymouth Sound. It was built as a 'ruin' out of the remains of a mediaeval chapel in nearby Stonehouse. Its spiral staircase leads to another excellent vantage point over the Sound. It is said that there was once an obelisk on this site, believed to have been erected by Lady Edgcumbe in memory of her pet pig called 'Cupid'.

Just above the folly is the Great Terrace, or Earl's Drive, a carriageway which ran from the house around the contours of the coastline. It affords a lovely walk to the two villages of Kingsand and Cawsand, small twin villages divided by a stream that runs under Garett Street. Historically Kingsand and Mount Edgcumbe were part of Devon until 1844, a stone marker on a house still shows this ancient divide. The walk from Cremyll to these villages is about three miles but there is a bus service back to Cremyll if the spirit is willing but the flesh is weak.

The two communities once thrived on the maritime activities of pilchard-fishing and smuggling. It was reckoned, in the early nineteenth century, that many thousands of barrels of 'stingo' (illicitly imported liquor) were landed in little Cawsand Bay.

There is far more to this 'Plymouth' countryside beyond the Tamar, more subtleties than you would perchance to dream and, as it is so open, it begs to be explored. You may even discern the sounds of boats being lovingly built at Mashford's Boat Yard, a short distance away, where *Gipsy Moth* was built for Sir Francis Chichester.

Up river on the opposite side of the 'Hamoaze' (the mouth of the Tamar) much bigger vessels are built or maintained at the world famous Devonport Dockyards.

Soon after his arrival in England in 1688, William of Orange recognised the strategic importance of Plymouth's location in relation to France, his enemy, and supported the development of the settlement called Plymouth Dock. However, as a creek and marshland separated it from the old fishing port of Plymouth, the locals disassociated their own town by dropping 'Plymouth' and simply called it 'Dock'. By 1821 it was far bigger than Plymouth and, with its fine buildings and attractive layout, it merited a name worthy of its status. From 1 January 1824 it became Devonport, the port of Devon, and the celebrations were colourful and prolonged – there were numerous feasts and parties.

John Foulston, a brilliant architect, designed the Town Hall in Ker Street, a copy of the

Parthenon crowned with a figure of Britannia. Beside it rose a 125 foot high granite memorial column to celebrate the arrival of Devonport. Beside this was the Neo-Egyptian military library, complete with its collection of four thousand books. All these gems were reached at the end of a Foulston designed terrace. They must have been heady days for Devonport!

Sadly the terrace of elegant buildings which led up to the Town Hall were allowed to decay and were demolished by those unenlightened souls who opted for 'sterile' rather than 'style'. The Egyptian styled library is now licensed premises and Foulston's architecture seems totally out of place in an area given to accommodating people in skyward-stretching stacks.

The many thousands of people who go on the hour long voyage to see the Navy ships don't get to see the town of Devonport. They will see England's glory but the yards, the gantries and Devon's version of the former Berlin Wall, veil the twilight town of Devonport. This perimeter wall surrounds a vast area of docks and it has even impinged onto Devonport's main street. Fore Street was the heart of the town with its hotels, cinemas and theatres. Following extensive bombing by the Luftwaffe during the Second World War, the Admiralty seized more than fifty acres of land which included the lower half of Fore Street, the heart and pulse of Devonport. A wall was put up and has proved to be divisive for, even now, there are buildings and memories on the other side of the wall

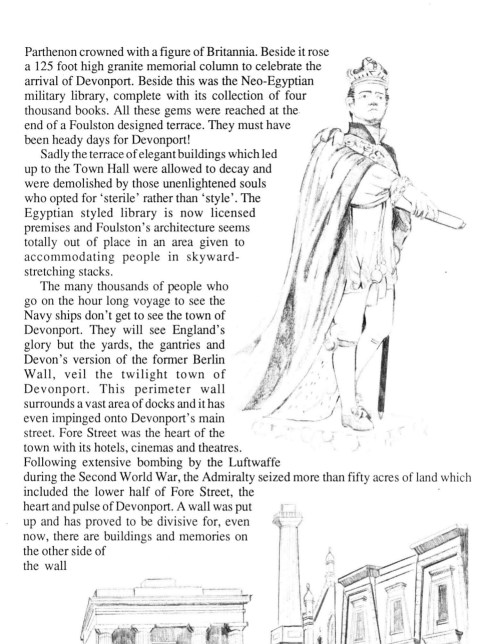

unseen by residents for generations. There is the premises of FST, the 'Fifty Shillings Tailors' who would run you up a fine suit so durable that you could buy it for your wedding, wear it for Sunday best, and still be the smartest dressed (hopefully, many decades later) at your own funeral! Beside that is the building which was 'Marks and Sparks'. In its heyday it was brightly decorated with gold and purple cladding yet that has gone now and it is somewhat anaemic-looking, its lifeblood apparently drained as it acts as a store in the other sense of the word. Nearby is the Midland Bank building complete with its '1922' proudly over the door, another bank clearly overdrawn on its original use. There was also a market, a real lively affair where multitudes gathered to haggle over the first fruits of the season from the Tamar Valley – raspberries, strawberries, cherries or apples. The market, which was so lively and was such a mecca for the local populous when it was in its prime, is now encased in this sort of ghost town, once Devonport's pride and joy.

In recent years we have seen what a wonderful job has been done to landscape the city centre of Plymouth so perhaps it is time to roll up the sleeves and address the problems of Devonport. For the record, Devonport became a part of Plymouth in 1914 at a time when the latter's population had outstripped the former's, otherwise 'Devonport' would most probably have been the adopted name for the overall settlement.

Plymouth people are greatly influenced by Cornwall. The counties are linked by ferry, by floating bridge, by viaducts and

by road bridges. However it was not until the great genius of Isambard Kingdom Brunel was put to work that a speedy and safe link could be forged between Devon and Cornwall. Brunel was involved in many engineering works locally and was instrumental in the development of Millbay Docks. He brought the railway down to the waterside and in so doing skillfully negotiated some tricky gradients. For good measure he also planned a floating dock at Sutton Harbour and lock gates for the side of West Pier. These last measures remained in the planning stage. But it is his Royal Albert Bridge across the Tamar to Saltash which is an enduring masterpiece of engineering.

Brunel submitted two possible plans, one a single span and the other a double. The latter was less expensive but, once it had been accepted that this was the way to span the Tamar, Brunel still had to overcome both natural and man-made problems. The Admiralty insisted that the bridge must be at least a hundred feet clear of the water to allow ships to pass upstream. In the bed of the seventy foot deep river there was another seventy feet of mud. Brunel applied his great knowledge to the task in hand and the bridge took shape. The two centre spans are 455 feet long and were swung into place to within a tenth of an inch of accuracy which, considering the limitations of Victorian technology, was almost a miracle. A crowd estimated at about fifty thousand strong came to witness this spectacle.

When complete, the Royal Albert Bridge had cost a staggering quarter of a million pounds and had used some four thousand tons of iron. It needs painting about every five or six years, and has been the star of quite a few television commercials, Unfortunately Brunel missed the opening ceremony, performed by Prince Albert; as the first train made its way towards Truro on 11 April 1859, Brunel lay ill in Switzerland. However he made it back to England and, a short time before his death, at the age of fifty three, he was taken over his bridge in a specially adapted carriage.

To show recognition for this great bridge the railway authorities had Brunel's name and the date 1859 put at each end of the bridge. There is a commemorative plaque to him alongside the railway on the Devon side of his railway bridge, just below the bridge car park.

The Tamar Bridge opened in 1961 replacing a ferry service which had existed for a long time. The floating bridges could not cope with the traffic levels and the toll bridge was the only answer. It was opened by HM Queen Elizabeth the Queen Mother, and when it reached twenty five years of service she wrote a congratulatory letter.

The traffic which goes up and down the Tamar is considerably less than that which crosses it. To go up river is to get away from life in the fast lane in exchange for some great countryside. A short distance upstream the River Tavy adds its considerable flow to the

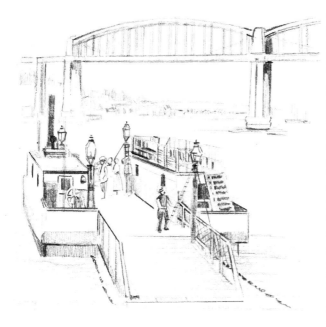

waters of the Tamar. It is a river which rises high on the moor not far from its most remote tor, Fur Tor. It then falls with remarkable steepness, for a Devonshire river, from its moorland tableland in a succession of rapids and waterfalls. It gives its name to Mary and Peter Tavy and, of course, to Tavistock. Beneath the latter it enters into a deep, wooded and beautiful valley. Its estuary, like many in South Devon, is comparatively short. Lopwell Dam, created to boost Plymouth's ever increasing thirst for water, is where the river starts to show its estuary-like features. This is a beauty spot and when the tide is out people like to explore this Tavy Country.

In one of the feeder valleys lies Milton Combe, a small village almost completely enfolded within the hills. To use brochure type jargon it is 'quaint', a most unlikely spot

so close to a major conglomeration of people but so rural in its appearance. The surprise of finding this type of settlement is mirrored in the pub's name – the 'Who'd Have Thought It'. The story goes that there was an inn in the village but another villager didn't like its landlord so applied for a licence to open his own place as a pub. After growing accustomed to his many applications being turned down, when the postman eventually delivered the good news, 'Who'd Have Thought It!' were his words of surprise. The pub has gone from strength to strength and is now the only one in the village. It possesses a ghost called 'Abe', a colourful Royalist Cavalier complete with uniform. He has been seen on several occasions by various locals and usually at night.

A short distance away is Buckland Abbey, owned by the National Trust since 1948. Much work has been done to make it the showpiece that it deserves to be, in true National Trust traditions, of course. Apart from its shop there are many things to savour as the whole place reflects its great links with Sir Francis Drake. By buying it, in 1581, he created a home to return to in the same area where he had been born. His birthplace was at Crowndale on the outskirts of Tavistock, some three or four miles upstream. Although he had left here at an early age to grow up on the Medway Estuary in Kent, and despite the fact that he had gone all over the globe, he realised that to return to his roots was a sensible notion. Naturally there are many artifacts of the great man and the buildings themselves are a great attraction. Drake's Drum remains poised to beat if the country is threatened again. Hopefully, it will remain as silent as it must have been when Buckland Abbey was founded as a Cistercian Monastery in 1278. At the Dissolution it fell into private hands with Sir Richard Grenville eventually selling it to Drake.

The *Treasure Hunt* TV programme, which began on Plymouth's Breakwater, successfully ended at Buckland Abbey with Anneka Rice breathlessly speaking those immortal words, 'Stop the clock – I've found it!' A tiny replica of Drake's Drum signalled the end of a glorious journey o v e r

most of the countryside traversed in this little book.

We must end our brief look at Plymouth by returning to the banks of the river which takes its name, so philologists believe, from the number of plum farms that were where modern Plympton is today. On the banks of the Plym, and within the city limits, is Saltram House, set in three hundred acres of attractive parkland. Owned and managed by the National Trust, it is a fine eighteenth century house which, in the morning light, gleams

majestically white and bright. Within there is a fine collection of Sir Joshua Reynolds' paintings – he was a friend of the Parker family who resided there. Sir Joshua was the son of the vicar of Plympton St Maurice and master of Plympton Grammar School, and Joshua had the honour of being its mayor in 1773.

The library at Saltram House is another of its features but this *Great Little Plymouth Book* is not part of that collection – it is for you to enjoy and savour and to add to your own collection. We hope that you enjoyed it!